Parkinson's Disease

How to Talk About it with Your Kids

ROBERT L. LINDSAY

Copyright © 2019 Robert L. Lindsay

All Rights Reserved

ISBN: 9781793019004

No part of this book may be reproduced or transmitted in any form or by any means, electronic or mechanical, including photocopying, recording or by any information storage and retrieval system, without written permission from the author.

Disclaimer

This book is not meant to be used, nor should it be used, to diagnose or treat any medical condition. For diagnosis or treatment of any medical problem, consult your own physician. The publisher and author are not responsible for any specific health needs that may require medical supervision and are not liable for any damages or negative consequences from any treatment, action, application or preparation, to any person reading of following the information in this book. References are provided for informational purposes only and do not constitute endorsement or advocacy.

Acknowledgements

This book would not have been possible without the support and encouragement from so many friends and colleagues. These are the people who made this book much more than the work of the guy whose name appears on the cover; these are the individuals who shared their talents, their time, and their expertise to ensure that this story is told accurately, thoroughly, and well.

I am indebted to Dr. Anthony Fredericks, for holding my literary hand and guiding me down new paths to learn the power of support, encouragement, and direction in effectively dealing with a challenging medical condition.

To David and Lauren Ohl, my heartfelt appreciation for sharing the story of their family and enlightening others as to the positive power of communication in dealing with an ailment that both consumes and confuses. Their strength and determination is truly reflected in the pages of this book.

To my family – Susan, Brian, and Kevin for their love and support.

To my many friends, medical team members, and college family members, including: Dr. Mike McGough, Dr, Alex Pantelyat, Mr. Pete Petemeier, Dr. Kim Sutton, Mr. Jay Allen, Mr. Art Guyer, Mr. Warren Risk, Ms. Delayne McWilliams, Dr. John Spence, Mr. Dave Scarborough, Mr. Tom (TA)

Anderson, Mr. Tom Ellis, Dr. Terry Evans, Mr. George Suder, Mr. Gary Hartman, Mike and Kathy Wark, Mr. Hank Sinkey, Mr. Rick Morgan, Dr. Eric Ling, Claudia Fanning, Dr. Lee Fanning and Dr. Dan Hans. They provided specific review/feedback, words of encouragement and a whole lot of literary love!

To Sue

my beautiful wife and best friend

Contents

Foreword, *Anthony Fredericks* i

Introduction 1

1 | Strategies to Share 7

2 | Preschoolers: 3-6 Years 13

3 | School-age: 6-12 Years 17

4 | Adolescents: 12-18 Years 23

5 | College and Beyond 27

6 | Knowledge is Power 31

7 | The Parkinson's Primer 35

Additional Resources 39

Foreword

Shortly after Bob Lindsay was diagnosed with Parkinson's Disease, he went through the usual stages of disbelief, denial, anger, and confusion. As a former basketball player in college, he always kept himself in good shape and excellent health, but now his body was in revolt – a full-scale rebellion from which there was no retreat! He also knew that his life – and the lives of those around him – would be forever altered. It was then that his oldest son, Brian, gave him a copy of Michael J. Fox's bestselling book, *Always Looking Up: The Adventures of an Incurable Optimist* (New York: Hachette Books, 2010).

His life changed!

Reading *Always Looking Up,* Bob gained a fresh perspective – the book was both uplifting and instructive. It also reinforced the power of one individual's initiative to improve the lives of others. Interestingly, it was bibliotherapy in reverse: a child informing a parent through a book. On one hand, it uniquely underscored the power of family to make a difference. On the other hand, it rejuvenated and reinforced the basic core of Bob's personality.

In 2003, Bob was recruited to join the Department of Education at York College of Pennsylvania. His expertise in the field of special education was just what undergraduate students needed as they prepared for their careers as future classroom teachers. I was well-acquainted with Bob's personality and positive outlook on life long before he joined the faculty (His reputation preceded him). The fact that he and I shared the same birthday (February 25) notwithstanding, we hit it off on both a professional and personal level. I enjoyed his unique sense of humor, his breadth of knowledge, his respect for others, and his constant *joie de vivre*. Those were the same qualities he brought to all his undergraduate classes. Students constantly commented (in post-semester evaluations) that Professor Lindsay "was sincerely dedicated to the academic success of every student," "went out of his way to ensure that we learned what we needed to learn," and "made every class an unmissable class."

Bob's office and mine were side by side and we frequently shared anecdotes, solicited professional advice from each other, and worked in concert on several curricular initiatives. His spirit was always there: a unique combination of positive energy, professional respect, and innovative ideas.

However, the ravages of the disease were taking their toll and Bob officially retired from college teaching in 2015. Later, upon my own retirement in 2017, I was invited to join a small group of recently retired educators (including Bob), who meet every six weeks at a local café for a three-hour breakfast to discuss and solve all the problems of the world (We are affectionately known as R.O.M.E.O.s [**R**etired **O**ld **M**en **E**ating **O**ut]). Every time we get together, Bob's spirit is always sparkling – consistently upbeat and continually inspirational.

During this time, Bob kept in constant contact with his two children. Once, while playing a popular board game called Cranium ("The Game for Your Whole Brain"), he was paired with his younger son, Kevin. Kevin began to notice how his father's cognitive skills seemed to be somewhat delayed and his ability to respond and interact with him was slower and more labored. The opportunity to discuss these changes honestly was helpful in assisting Kevin to better understand some of the conditions his father deals with on a regular basis. Those discussions have created closer family bonds and deeper appreciation for Bob's day-to-day challenges.

Now, it's your turn to experience Bob's wisdom, his dedication to friends and family, his calming and contemplative demeanor, and his steadfast devotion to improving the lives of others. This book will give you answers to many unanswered questions. It will help you communicate with your children and invite them into a loving circle of support, engagement, and positivity. With this book, you'll be able to talk with your children in ways that will help them understand and deal with a family member who has Parkinson's. It will answer their questions as much as it will answer yours. In a way, you will be changed and so will your children... all for the better.

—Anthony D. Fredericks, Ed.D.
Professor of Education (retired)
York College of Pennsylvania

Introduction

"In hindsight, there could have been more time together. You can never have too much love and family togetherness."

Dave and Lauren have three kids - Ryan, Alexandra, and Cami. Dave's father, Jerry, was diagnosed with Parkinson's Disease (PD) at age 62 - when the kids were young and unaware of what the disease was or of its debilitating progression to come. Their parents admitted they were guilty of the universal parental "fault" - protecting their kids: waiting until they were old enough to understand what the disease was doing and what it might mean for family gatherings and celebrations. But they also knew there was some necessary education...some explanations wrapped in emotions that were often indescribable, fragile, and powerful.

"At diagnosis, the kids were too young to address it with them. The symptoms were very slight and we did not discuss it at the time. The serious discussions came as the kids got older and symptoms became more pronounced. The ages of the kids were a big factor for us in how the conversations evolved. We strived to be proactive in telling the kids what to expect when they saw Grandpa, and how they could help. This seemed to us a more age-appropriate approach than announcing Grandpa had a disease that would rob him physically and mentally in a slow painful process. We wanted to educate them, but not scare them. As the kids got older the questions became more difficult. A very heavy 'Is Grandpa going to be OK?' and even heavier 'Is Grandpa going to die?' are questions that eventually would be asked with more frequency."

"We wanted to give them, over time, a little of what they needed to know. We wanted to share some of the symptoms and what those symptoms meant in their dealings with their grandfather. Those things could include: his attention span, that he needed help when getting out of a chair, his trouble with walking, how they could help him into and out of a car, and other things they could do to assist him. But, we were also sensitive to how the kids would handle it. We were in uncharted territory."

Dave and Lauren, like tens of thousands of parents around the country, had come up against an element of parenting rarely discussed in parenting books and rarely shared in conversations during family gatherings. This was new ground and they were often treading on proverbial eggshells when talking about the slow and inevitable progression of the disease. In so many ways, they had to fly by the seat of their pants - using their instincts and their intimate knowledge of each child's personality to reveal only "what they could handle at the time."

"The kids were sensitive enough to know that their grandfather was fragile and he was getting more so the older he got and the older they became. For some reason, we're not sure what, we had a tendency to focus more on the symptoms rather than the actual disease. We seldom used the word 'Parkinson's' or the word 'disease.' The kids were aware of the symptoms; they could see those symptoms displayed every time they visited their grandfather. So, they sort of led the way and that was the way we wanted to keep it. It was less painful for the kids and because of the slow progression of Parkinson's we could share its effects over a longer period of time. It wasn't so shocking for them."

Dave and Lauren wrestled with an issue far too many parents confront as they seek ways to share information about the disease with their children. They fretted about what to share and when to share it. But, as in many familial challenges, it was their kids who led the way. The kids' questions focused on their grandfather's symptoms and the changes in those symptoms over a long progression of time. Dave and Lauren took the time to talk candidly and honestly about those symptoms that were clearly visible in Jerry and, just as important, how their children could respond to those symptoms. This was an exercise in familial communication and conversation that offered their kids an entrée into a fact of life that was clearly evident in every visit, family meal, or holiday celebration.

"The kids knew he was fragile, but we knew we couldn't stop communicating just because of the disease. We knew that Jerry could still internalize those emotions and to isolate the kids from that interactive process would have been unfair to Jerry. For us, the continual communication between the grandchildren and their grandfather was critical. That may involve personal visits, digital visits via FaceTime and Skype, emails and tweets, or simply old-fashioned phone calls. Somehow, we just knew that continuous communication was the key."

Dave and Lauren put it best when they said, "We knew that we wanted to do as much as we could before the disease got too bad. For us, it was quality time spent together – whether that time was just sitting down on the couch together to watch a baseball game on TV or holding hands while walking down the street or just having dinner together. It wasn't always the amount of words that were said, it was the time that was important."

There is often a mistaken belief that children should not be involved or should not be integrated into the trials and travails of Parkinson's. Part of that mindset rests on the assumption that kids cannot emotionally handle – over the long term – the debilitating effects of the disease on someone they love. In short, we often falsely believe that child-ren are not ready to face the emotional challenges that will often exacerbate and magnify as time goes on. The thinking is that Parkinson's is an adult disease and should only be handled by adults.

I believe that's wrong!

As a lifelong educator (and a Parkinson's patient), I have seen the positive effects on children's growth and development when they are included in discussions about, and family interactions over, a relative diagnosed with a debilitating disease. I also know from decades of educational research that children who grow up in families who spend time talking about emotions are academically more successful, have better friendships, and can handle difficult social situations more effectively than children whose families do not talk about feelings. By extension then, there is considerable evidence that a home environment in which children can freely express and share the emotional issues surrounding Parkinson's is a supportive one. That environment recognizes that children succeed on many fronts when they have opportunities to articulate ideas, convey feelings, and receive constant support as they grow older and deal with the more complex issues related to a debilitating disease such as Parkinson's.

Merely observing and taking note of children's emotions (and their expression of those emotions) surrounding a family member with Parkinson's sets a foundation for some powerful discussions. That foundation helps us recognize that children's emotional expressions are a familial opportunity for closer bonding. That bonding becomes a positive experience in their lives – letting children know that we hear them and that we understand their feelings. These are what teachers call "teachable moments" – times when an unexpected or unplanned situation pops up… an event from which children can learn an important lesson. ("I know you're sad when Gramps can't go on walks with you, but sometimes his body doesn't work the way he would like.") The simple act of recognizing that something is different is grounds for family discussions and the opening up of emotions that are not always pleasant, but certainly always necessary.

Let's begin those discussions with some universal strategies appropriate for any family and any family situation.

Chapter 1

Strategies to Share

Here are some specific strategies to share with your children... no matter what their age:

1. Kids often have some conflicting issues and information about health issues. We often talk about "catching a cold" or "getting a disease." As a result, young children (particularly) may believe that all diseases are "caught" or "transmitted. It is vitally important that kids know that Parkinson's is NOT a communicable or contagious disease – it cannot be passed along from someone who has it to another. It is perfectly safe to be with or touch someone who has PD. You can help your children understand this concept by modeling "touching behaviors" (e.g. holding hands, hugs, embraces, simple massage, stroking, etc.) frequently with a PD

patient. With very young children (who are more impressionable) take the time to talk about what you are doing ("I'm holding Uncle Brandon's hand to show how much I care").

2. Regardless of your child's age, your emphasis should be on acknowledgement and reassurance. Don't "sweep the disease under the rug" – rather, be honest with your children that someone they love has an affliction and that the affliction often manifests itself in outward physical signs such as tremors, rigidity, and instability. Kids will notice, for example, any physical shaking, thus raising their level of concern. Take the time to talk about the outward signs of PD as well as their inner feelings in response to those manifestations.

3. Be prepared to repeat yourself – particularly with specific vocabulary. There are certain terms used quite frequently in any discussions of Parkinson's. Don't "hide" those words from your children; instead help your children understand what those words mean... in language they can understand. For example, you may describe a tremor as "when the brain makes the body shake for no reason." Later, you may tell your kids that a tremor is when "someone's body jiggles like a bowl of Jell-O." Invite your children to ask for clarification or repetition ("Tell me the part you know").

4. Let your children know that a Parkinson's patient will have her or his "ups and downs" (like a see-saw). It is important your children know that there will be a mix of feelings and emotions as an adult deals with the cumulative effects of Parkinson's. It's equally important that all feelings are acknowledged as they emerge. Artificially suppressing those feelings ("There, there, you shouldn't cry just because Grandma fell down") will actually do more harm than good.

5. One of the most successful ways of inviting your children into the conversation is through the use of bibliotherapy. Bibliotherapy is the process of using children's literature to help kids think about, understand, and work through social and emotional concerns – most often in a casual and unstructured conversation. A book can serve as a means for family members to discuss sensitive issues and help children understand the challenges associated with PD. As a parent, you can use reading to help your kids come to grips with issues that may create emotional turmoil for them. Here are a few suggested books (check with the children's librarian at your local public library for more titles):

- Ali, Rasheda. *I'll Hold Your Hand So You Won't Fall: A Child's Guide to Parkinson's Disease.* (West Palm Beach, FL: Merit Publishing, 2010).

- Hultquist, A. *A Day with Parkinson's.* (Park Ridge, IL: Albert Whitman and Co., 2016).

- Jenkins, Kay. *Who is Pee Dee? Explaining Parkinson's to a Child.* (Atlanta, GA: UCB, Inc., 2008).

- Silverstein, Alvin. *Parkinson's Disease.* (New York, NY: Enslow Publishers, 2002).

6. One of the most important ways we can communicate with our children is through modeling. What this means, quite simply, is that you describe your actions orally as you perform an activity with a Parkinson's patient ("I'm now going to hold Grandpa's arm so he can walk across the room without falling").

Good modeling is a combination of visual cues and talking while your kids watch and listen ("Let's both hold Aunt Barbara's hands so she can get up out of her chair"). This technique can be very effective in helping kids understand the everyday challenges of PD. Through your modeling, your youngsters can become more active in understanding more about the disease.

7. Non-verbal communication can be as important as verbal communication. The way you stand, sit, or greet another person of any age, conveys subtle messages about your expectations and attitudes. When you smile at your father (who has PD) whenever he enters the room sends an important message to your child. When you sit close to your grandmother (who has PD) every time you visit also gives your children some important clues.

8. Perhaps, most important of all, encourage questions and help your children feel comfortable in seeking answers to those questions. Family discussions, casual conversations, looking up information on the internet, and reading books together are all ways in which children can satisfy their natural curiosity about this disease that is affecting someone they love. Don't discourage these searches for answers; rather, work together with your children to seek answers. Offer them avenues of discovery – appropriate for their age – avenues that invite them to learn and understand.

According to David and Lauren, "Learning about disease and death is one of the biggest life lessons parents can teach and experience with their children. Keeping the lines of communication open is an enormous factor in a child's ability to process and fully understand losing a family member. We found speaking all together was beneficial, rather than individually with the kids (despite age differences). Oftentimes, one child would ask a question the others either didn't think of, or were too nervous to ask. It helps everyone throughout the entire process to have an ongoing, open discussion. Children will inevitably surprise you with their insightfulness and willingness to help."

Not surprisingly, many parents worry over what is actually appropriate for the age of their children. The following chapters offer specific information recommended for various age groups.

Chapter 2

Preschoolers: 3 to 6 years

Youngsters are at the stage of life where they are trying to make sense of the world: there's a lot of incoming information... not all of it is immediately comprehensible. And, as you well know, kids at this age have an abundance of questions: "Why is the sky blue?" "Where do babies come from?" and "Why does Uncle Bill have such a big belly?" are typical of the innocent queries your children pose at this age. It's their way of trying to make sense of a wider world – a world beyond their bedroom or backyard. Some of those questions, as any parent of a four-year-old will tell you, can be difficult to answer ("Why do people have to die?"). Here are some suggestions for communicating with youngsters at this age:

- Ask your preschooler questions about a family member who has PD. This has the advantage of letting kids know that it is OK to talk about people who are "different." Questions such as, "What did you notice about Grandpa today?" "What did you see Mother do when she was in the kitchen?" and "What did you and Granny do together at her house?" Notice that the emphasis in these questions is just on gathering factual information – giving you some insights on how your child might be perceiving or interpreting specific aspects of PD.

- Encourage your children to talk about their feelings. What are they thinking? How do they feel? What is scary? What do they see? They may express some fears or uncertainties. That's perfectly normal. But, you need to be aware of those fears and uncertainties so that you can assure your children that they are perfectly normal. This opens the door to letting children know that you, too, have some fears and uncertainties. And, that's OK. Children need the reassurance that their fears and uncertainties are not uncommon – we all have them to one degree or another.

- Take time to have one-on-one conversations with your children. Pay attention to them and make them feel as though they are the only other person in the room when they speak to you. Make sure the conversation takes place in a relaxed atmosphere (no TV, computer, or other family members) and encourage them to open up to you.

- Let your children know that feelings can be positive, negative, or somewhere in-between. At this age they are wrestling with newfound feelings and emotions. Some will be positive (They built a tower that is eleven blocks high.); some will be negative (Their brother knocks over the tower.); and some will be in-between (Their brother knocks over part of the tower, but helps to put it back together). Talking about both feelings is both healthy and necessary for the growth and development of any child.

EXAMPLE:

Your child notices that Grandpa is shuffling his feet. There is a confused look on his face. What can you say and do?

Parent: Sweetie, you have a sad look on your face. Tell me why.

Child: Grandpa is walking funny. Not the way he usually does.

Parent: Does that make you feel sad?

Child: Yeah. He looks different and he walks different.

Parent: Sometimes he'll do that. It's just that his brain doesn't always send the right signals to his feet.

Child: Will he always do that?

Parent: Sometimes he will and sometimes he won't. Sometimes that makes me sad too. But, you know what? Sometimes it's OK to feel sad about someone else. Remember when you fell off the slide? I got sad, too. But, then, the next day I was happy again.

Chapter 3

School-age: 6-12 years

Children in grades 1–6 are more sophisticated about language and communication skills. Their thought processes are more comprehensive, they are becoming more aware of the world around them, and they ask (not always aloud) considerably more questions in trying to make some sense of that world ("Mommy, did you ever want to get a tattoo?").

Similarly, school-age children are most sensitive about feelings and emotions. Not only have they experienced a wider range of feelings by this age, they are also developing some questions about those emotions ("good" emotions; "bad" emotions). This is the time in their lives when conversations should be frequent, regular, and sustained. For example, kids (just like us) have "bad days." Rather than bottling up those feelings inside they need a vent – a way to deal with, and begin to understand, those emotions. It's vitally critical that your children feel a level of comfort in sharing those emotions with an understanding adult.

"I got scared when Daddy just stared at me for a long time without saying anything." Not discussing this or saying something like, "That's OK," does little to assuage a child's feelings. On the other hand, a follow-up question such as, "What frightened you the most?" lets the child know you have acknowledged his or her feelings and are willing to discuss them in an age-appropriate manner.

- Keep lines of communication open at this stage of their lives. Your children are expanding their personal horizons at this stage – they take on new friends and develop new relationships with a wider circle of acquaintances. Keep talking with your child on a daily basis – what do you and your friends do, talk about, or are learning (in or out of school)? What do you like or not like?

- It's critical that your children know you are always there with age-appropriate answers to their questions. They will, quite naturally, turn to their friends and classmates to obtain answers (often incorrect) to worrisome statements like "Yeah, your grandpa is stumbling a lot because he's going to die soon!" Keep the conversations about a family member with PD open and ongoing so that, if and when changes occur, your child is comfortable in asking for the most correct and appropriate information.

- Children at this age need reasons and rationale for why things happen as they do. Telling your children that Mommy sometimes freezes is insufficient. They want to know why. Sharing something like, "Sometimes the signals from Mommy's brain don't always work right," would be an appropriate way to explain a behavior. Obviously, long scientific or medical explanations are unnecessary as well as inappropriate. Use vocabulary well within your child's level of comprehension.

- Sometimes children at this age feel guilty when things around them go wrong. They need to get regular messages from adults that it is not their fault that a parent or relative has Parkinson's. What they do (or don't do) is not a factor in either the onset or progression of the disease. In short, they are not to blame.

- Always talk with your child in a calm voice. Getting agitated or upset may be counterproductive to helping your child understand the connection between what happens and its reason. A frustrated or angry tone of voice always sends the wrong message to children – it says that they, too, should be frustrated or angry, when compassion and patience may be most necessary.

- Encourage children to talk about their feelings or emotions as well as the reasons why those emotions are occurring. These conversations should be regular, frequent and comfortable. Most important, don't interrupt children when they are trying to tell you something. They need to feel comfortable in sharing their feelings without condemnation or judgment.

EXAMPLE:

Your nine-year-old daughter comes home from school and says that some of the kids on the playground were making fun of your husband because he's only 48 years old and has to use a cane to get around.

Child: Hey, Mommy, the girls at school were saying that Daddy is a really old man because he has to use a cane.

Parent: How did that make you feel?

Child: I got really angry and told them that they didn't know what they were talking about.

Parent: So, you got really upset when other kids said something bad about your father?

Child: Yeah.

Parent: Why do you think you got so upset?

Child: Well, Daddy isn't an old man. He just has that Parkinson's Disease that sometimes makes him walk in a strange way.

Parent: Yeah, like we talked earlier, he has Parkinson's. Sometimes the disease makes people do things out of the ordinary and other people don't always understand.

Child: Yeah, they don't know anything about Daddy or his disease.

Parent: You're probably right. So, what do you think you should do?

Child: Maybe they should read a book or something. Or maybe we could share some information in class someday.

Parent: Yeah, those both sound like good ideas.

Chapter 4

Adolescents: 12 to 18 years

Adolescence is a time for self-discovery as well as a time of great social conflict. Emotions are often raw and feelings are easily bruised. Adolescents want to know who they are and how they "compare" with their peers. Not surprisingly, adolescents frequently have negative views about themselves and the world in which they live. Conflicts with parents and conflicts with classmates are not uncommon and many will spend considerable amounts of time by themselves wrestling with a mishmash of raw emotions. It is critical, perhaps more than ever before, to keep the discussions going and the wheels of communication well-oiled.

- Be sensitive and responsive to the adolescent experience. At this age your children are going through great changes and there are more "unknowns" than "knowns." They need to know that they can share their thoughts without triggering adults "who want to jump down their throats."

- At this time in their life, adolescents want to feel independent; yet at the same time, they often fight with themselves and others. Don't judge and don't condemn. Give your children the freedom (and the comfortableness) to express themselves in a non-judgmental atmosphere. This is a time of considerable angst and uncertainty – and support, rather than condemnation, is always preferred.

- Adolescents need to know they are connected with the family. Communications initiated and maintained throughout their young lives will have much to say about how well they are able to deal with some of the mixed feelings often associated with this age group. Continue to ask questions of your children, continue to respond to queries, and continue to show them that the lines of communication are always open and available.

- Give them space. Sometimes your children just need some time to deal with issues in their own way. That doesn't mean they're shunning the family – it just means they need an unstressed opportunity to sort through conflicting emotions and feelings. It's important to let them know you are there (in the background) for any requested ideas and counsel.

- Employ good listening strategies. Demonstrate through your body language and facial expressions that you are "with them" as they ask tough questions and search for tough answers. Judgments and accusations have no place in these conversations.

- Don't be adverse to using professional services. Adolescents sometimes need professional counseling to help them deal with a parent or relative who has Parkinson's. There is no stigma to seeking professional help – it is, most assuredly, a sign of strength to obtain some outside advice or opinions.

EXAMPLE:

Your 14-year-old son notices that his grandmother often has an expressionless face when he visits her house on holidays and family celebrations.

Child: Hey, Dad, what's going on with Grandma?

Parent: Remember all those talks we had about Parkinson's Disease?

Child: Yeah!

Parent: Remember when I told you that as the disease progresses a person sometimes loses some bodily functions?

Child: Yeah, now I remember. So this is one of those times when Grandma can't control her body?

Parent: Yes. But, I'm curious, how does that make you feel?

Child: I feel really bad. She seems to have trouble getting around and she's not as active as she used to be.

Parent: Well, those are natural reactions. Those are some of the same feelings your mother and I have. It's perfectly normal to feel that way.

Child: Yeah, I know it is. I just wish Grandma could be the way she was when we spent that summer at the shore.

Parent: Yeah, that was some fun! And, that will always be a good memory to keep.

Chapter 5

College and Beyond

At the beginning of each semester, I explained to members of my undergraduate classes that I had Parkinson's Disease. I gave what I thought was a realistic description of the main characteristics of Parkinson's. The students could see that, with medication, my motor functions were under control. Inadvertently, during one class, I heard a voice from the back say, "How can the man drive an hour each day to work with all of that going on!" And then, "I will not ride with him to my teaching assignment at Pleasant Acres School."

Since the student in question was an advisee of mine, I informally met with her after class to follow up on those comments. She told me that her grandfather had an advanced stage of Parkinson's and, as a result, she had read an online article with the following information:

> *Parkinson's disease is a type of movement disorder that can significantly impair driving skills, cause safety concerns, and force many people with the condition to stop driving a car. That's because the primary symptoms of Parkinson's disease can seriously interfere with the complex task of driving a car. Many people with early Parkinson's disease can safely continue driving, especially if symptoms are controlled. Because Park-*

> inson's disease worsens over time, however, many people with Parkinson's disease eventually will need to give up driving a car and rely on other forms of transportation.

Obviously, she thought I was more advanced in my Parkinson's progression and had a real concern about my capabilities... or lack of capabilities.

In this age of social media, college students and other young adults get much of their information from the internet as well as from friends, casual acquaintances, and total strangers. The proliferation of sites such as Facebook (1,710,000,000 monthly users), Twitter, LinkedIn, Snapchat, Instagram, Google+, Pinterest, and You Tube attest to the influence of electronic data on the daily lives of young people. As you are well aware, not all of that data is accurate, reliable, or trustworthy – but it is "absorbed" by a growing legion of impressionable minds. It is important, more than ever, to keep the familial conversations going.

- If you have a child in college, be sure to keep her or him constantly informed about the progression of the disease as it affects a loved one. Regularly mention how a patient is doing in your emails, Skype sessions, text messages, or other communiques with your youngster. Keep them informed.

- As you come across a significant article or web site (one that has been vetted by experts) be sure to pass it along to your college student. An article posted on the web site for the Parkinson's Foundation (http://www.parkinson.org), for example, would be most appropriate to share with your college student. An article that someone transmitted via Facebook may not be reliable or accurate and could, quite possibly, have erroneous information.

- As appropriate, offer opportunities for your college student to communicate with a loved one who has Parkinson's. Again, social media would be one way to foster open lines of communication. But, don't forget more traditional ways of communicating such as the phone or the postal service. Encourage regular opportunities to exchange information and you'll help your child "stay in touch."

- When your child comes home for semester breaks or vacations make some time for a "heart to heart" conversation about a loved one with Parkinson's. Don't ignore this family event by focusing solely on celebrations and holiday festivities. As always, it would be important to slot some time when family members can share and discuss current conditions at regular intervals.

- Your college student has many social, scholastic, and personal obligations as they progress through their education. It is critical that she or he is regularly informed and regularly engaged in family discussions, decisions, and deliberations. Keep the lines of communication open and ensure that your youngster is actively engaged in any events related to the PD patient.

Chapter 6

Knowledge is Power

In my discussions with professionals throughout the country, there is always a singular theme that comes up time and again. It was simply "Knowledge is power!" That certainly holds true in our adult lives as we deal with financial issues, personal relationships, occupational choices, and professional decisions. So, is it equally important in our children's lives... no matter what their age.

Kids are intuitive and they're also observant. They have a sense that something is different and something is out of the ordinary. Something doesn't look right or sound right ("How come Uncle Aaron never smiles?"). It is through those observations that they begin to generate questions and concerns. What is going on? What is happening? Ignoring that curiosity increases their anxiety levels. As parents, our challenge is to provide answers to those questions – answers that are developmentally appropriate for our children. One of the best ways to do that is by using "kid language" – words that come from your child's own natural speaking vocabulary... words and phrases she/he uses regularly with friends and classmates.

Here are a few examples:

- "The messages from Daddy's brain to his legs don't always get through."

- "Sometimes the way Aunt Betty looks is funny, but you know what, that's OK. That's who she is now."

- "Sometimes Grandmother's body feels like she has a lot of really sore muscles."

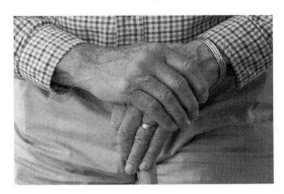

Another way is to use humor – a "light touch" often invites children to see another side of the disease. Psychologists sometimes define humor as "a painful thing told playfully" or a "tragedy separated by time and space." You will note that both definitions treat humor as a serious thought viewed in a light manner. Most important, humor (specifically, self-deprecating humor) helps make conversation (and the people conversing) more comfortable. Here are a few examples I have used:

- "Hey, how do you like my new dance steps?"

- "When I was your age we used to call this 'rock and roll'."

- "Would you like to shake my hand? Oh, never mind, it can do it by itself!"

But it is equally important that "kid language" and humor is balanced with an emphasis on the affective aspects of the disease. Parkinson's is a disease that exacts an emotional toll on all involved – especially children. We need to recognize that they have an emotional stake in any family members diagnosed with Parkinson's. As a result, it's important our children have an arena that encourages them to share their feelings and that their feelings are heard and recognized. This is not the time to criticize and condemn… it is the time to listen and respond with calmness and acceptance. The most important point we can make for kids is that an expression of feelings is always OK.

Chapter 7

The Parkinson's Primer

What You Need to Know

Below is a quick overview of Parkinson's Disease (PD). You are encouraged to consult other references for more detailed information and explanations (see the next section).

Brief Overview	Parkinson's Disease is a nervous system disorder. It is progressive (it gets worse as time goes on) and primarily affects movement. Tremors are common, as is stiffness and slowness of movement. Speech may be slurred. There is no cure, but certain medications improve the symptoms. One million Americans have the disease, with approximately 60,000 new patients diagnosed each year.
Causes	• Certain nerve cells in the brain break down or die. • A decrease in dopamine (a chemical in the brain that stimulates brain activity). • In rare cases, Parkinson's may be hereditary. • Environmental factors may increase the risk for Parkinson's.
Risk Factors	• It typically begins in middle age or late life.

	• Having many family members with the disease increases the risk. • Men are more prone to the disease than women. • Some pesticides and herbicides may increase one's risk.
Typical Symptoms	• Tremors • Slow movements • Muscle rigidity • Difficulty with balance • Speech changes • Slowed walking • Coordination problems • Apathy • Sleep disorders • Depression • Cognitive impairment • Stooped posture • Changes in writing
Complications	• Thinking difficulties • Chewing, eating, and swallowing problems • Sleep disorders • Bladder problems • Changes in blood pressure • Loss of smell • Fatigue

Talking with Kids: A Quick Review
In Chapter One I shared some specific strategies you should use in discussing Parkinson's Disease with children. Here they are again – albeit in a condensed format:

1.	Kids need to know (and understand) that Parkinson's IS NOT a communicable disease.
2.	When discussing Parkinson's with children be honest with them – acknowledge that someone has the disease; don't try to "hide" it from kids.
3.	Be sure children understand the meaning of certain words such as tremor, rigid, and balance (among others).
4.	Inform children that Parkinson's patients have good days and bad days (just like everybody else).
5.	Share children's literature about Parkinson's. Check with your local public library or your child's school librarian.
6.	As you interact with a Parkinson's patient, model the behaviors and attitudes you want children to practice.
7.	Remember that non-verbal communication (e.g. touching) is just as important as verbal communication.
8.	Encourage children to ask questions and then answer those questions promptly and honestly.

Additional Resources

How to Talk with Your Children about Parkinson's Disease (PD)

YouTube Videos

- Communicating with Children about Parkinson's
- Dad Living with Parkinson's
- Dave on Talking with Young Children About Mom's Parkinson's
- Explaining Parkinson's Disease to a Child
- Faces of Parkinson's
- How Parkinson's Disease Affects the Body – The Doctors
- People Over the World Talk about Their Parkinson's
- What Parkinson's Taught Me – Emma Lawton

Internet Articles

- *How to Talk with Your Kids about Parkinson's: Davis Phinney Foundation*
- *Parkinson's Disease – KidsHealth*
- *Talking to Children about Parkinson's – Parkinson's Foundation*
- *Talking to Children and Teenagers: Parkinson's UK*
- *Talking to Your Family about Parkinson's Disease – Healthline*

Books

A Parkinson's Primer: An Indispensable Guide to Parkinson's Disease for Patients and Their Families

Always Looking Up: The Adventures of an Incurable Optimist

Parkinson's Disease: A Complete Guide for Patients and Families

Understanding Parkinson's Disease: A Self-Help Guide (3rd edition)

About the Author

Robert L. Lindsay grew up in western Pennsylvania and then moved to south-central Pennsylvania in 1973. He obtained his bachelor's degree in Psychology from Washington and Jefferson College and his Master of Science Degree in Special Education and teaching certification from Clarion University. Shortly thereafter, he began work with the Lincoln Intermediate Unit as a special education specialist (Teacher, Instructional Advisor, Supervisor, and Assistant Director of Special Education) working with special needs children – a first career tallying 33 years. After his "retirement," he joined the Department of Education at York College of Pennsylvania where he taught undergraduate special education courses. A popular and celebrated lecturer, he was renowned for his personal and compelling anecdotes rooted in practical information and down-to-earth advice.

Lindsay was diagnosed with Parkinson's Disease in October of 2010. Since then, he has continued to educate others about Parkinson's – sharing not only what he has learned, but also his robust and positive spirit.